>> **CODE** POWER: **A TEEN PROGRAMMER'S GUIDE**™

GETTING TO KNOW

Ruby

HEATHER MOORE NIVER

rosen publishing's
rosen central®

NEW YORK

Published in 2015 by The Rosen Publishing Group, Inc.
29 East 21st Street, New York, NY 10010

First Edition

Library of Congress Cataloging-in-Publication Data

Niver, Heather Moore, author.
Getting to know Ruby/Heather Moore Niver.—First edition.
    pages cm.—(Code power: a teen programmer's guide)
Audience: Grades 5 to 8.
Includes bibliographical references and index.
ISBN 978-1-4777-7713-8 (library bound)—
ISBN 978-1-4777-7715-2 (pbk.)—
ISBN 978-1-4777-7716-9 (6-pack)
1. Ruby (Computer program language)—Juvenile literature.
2. Object-oriented programming (Computer science)—Juvenile literature. I. Title.
QA76.73.R83N58 2015
005.1'17—dc23
                                          2013049011

Manufactured in the United States of America

{ CONTENTS

Ruby is beautiful. Ruby is artful. Ruby is natural and clean. Lots of simple statements are bandied about to describe the coding language known as Ruby, but is it possible for a computer programming language to be all that? Many users seem to think it is. The language's creators want Ruby users to have a good time. In short, Ruby is made for programmer happiness.

With so many other programming languages already out there, though, who needs another one, no matter how cool? Well, Ruby stands out because it is consistent, elegant, and easy to use. For example, the following is a basic line of script that Larry Ullman, author of *Learn Ruby the Quick and Easy Way*, uses to show how clean Ruby code can be: Print "*Greetings, planet!*" Notice how easy that is. Ruby code doesn't bother with fancy tags, semicolons, or mysterious requests. The code is written in plain, direct language; by reading that script, the coder has a very good idea of what is going to happen when it runs. Ruby's creator, Yukihiro "Matz" Matsumoto, designed Ruby to be this clear.

Ruby is flexible. Because everything—yes, every last thing—in Ruby is an object (more on that later), users can change things. It's perfectly acceptable to download Ruby (for free, by the way), use it, and even change things around to suit whatever project is at hand. In fact, changing and playing around with Ruby is encouraged, as is posting creations on the Internet to share with other people.

>> Members of the group Ladies Learning Code in Toronto participate in an introductory Ruby class in 2011. Ruby is simple to learn and flexible for all kinds of projects.

Ruby is powerful as well. Ruby and Ruby on Rails, which is a web application framework that is coded in the Ruby language, are used to power and build websites that handle tremendous amounts of traffic every day. The online independent music site Pitchfork hums along because of Rails. Anyone who catches television shows on Hulu should thank Ruby on Rails, too.

When it's time to test out a code, Ruby shines. Ruby is rapid development programming, which means that when a programmer wants to test out code, he or she can easily try something new and see right away if it works. All a programmer needs to do is write the code, run it, change it (known as debugging), and run it again. If it works, great! If not, it's a piece of cake to try something else. And for anyone who is interested in programming, this is a whole lot of fun!

So the next time you want to look up a funky phrase in the Urban Dictionary or go to the *Guitar Hero* website, remember that these sites run thanks to Ruby and Ruby on Rails. Keep reading to learn more about natural, beautiful Ruby. And get ready for some programmer happiness.

CHAPTER 1

BEAUTIFUL, ARTFUL RUBY

Yukihiro "Matz" Matsumoto created Ruby by taking the best parts of other computer languages he liked, such as Perl, Smalltalk, Eiffel, Ada, and Lisp. He put them together to create one clean, natural language. In addition to being artful in this manner, Ruby is also useful and sensible. Matsumoto put a lot of thought into what he wanted from his new language. When he was done, he compared Ruby to the human body—simple on the outside, but complex within.

Ruby is a general, all-around programming language. It can be used to build websites, handle text, and even create games. Ruby has become one of the top ten most popular programming languages in the world according to the TIOBE Index, which measures how much programming languages grow.

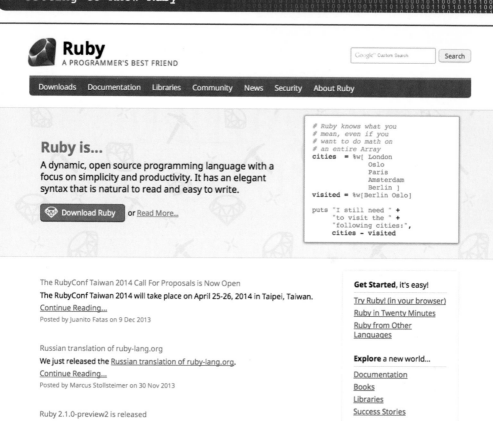

>> With the quick click of a mouse, Ruby can be downloaded—for free, in several different languages— and put to use in any number of projects.

OBJECT-ORIENTED CODE

Ruby is renowned for being an object-oriented programming language, but what does that mean? In any kind of programming language, all information or data is stored in a computer's memory. A collection of data is called an object. In most other languages, numbers are not considered objects. In Ruby everything is an object: every number, the smallest bit of information, and every fragment of code has its own instance variables (or properties) and methods (or actions). This is important because the programmer can treat every piece of information the same way.

An object can also be described as something that can perform a set of related activities. When a language is object-oriented, the user can change the objects to create and run a variety of programs.

Some of Ruby's muscle, suppleness, and ease of use also comes from the fact that it's an object-oriented programming (OOP) language. It is called a "pure" OOP language because every little thing in Ruby is an object. Other OOP languages have some objects or maybe even most things are objects, but not *everything*.

Being object-oriented means that Ruby programs tend to work the way the real world works. Programs understand and translate basic concepts and terms such as "ball," "people," and "car." An object-oriented language like Ruby makes it a cinch to use these concepts and base objects on them. Ruby understands and interprets the relationships between these terms and what they represent.

To anyone new to programming, it might seem obvious to use ideas from our lives in a computer program, but this is a relatively new concept in the software development world. Developed back in the 1960s, this concept didn't become popular until the 1990s. Languages that are not object-oriented don't give users

>> This is an avatar of Microsoft CEO Steve Ballmer "speaking" at the 2011 Consumer Electronics Show in Las Vegas. Object-oriented programming takes a term ("people") and makes it into an onscreen object (avatar).

as many choices when it comes to how they control concepts and how they connect.

WHAT'S SO GREAT ABOUT RUBY?

Ruby is sometimes compared to languages such as Python or Perl. With so many other programming languages out there, one might wonder why he or she should choose Ruby. One reason is that any type of program created can be written in Ruby. The language can be used for "text processing, system utilities, Web development, and even graphical applications," says author

Larry Ullman. The key is that Ruby coding is easy, flexible, natural, powerful, and clean.

EASY CODING

Quite simply, Ruby is easy to use. Other languages require special tags, complicated requests, or semicolons. Ruby's code is easy to read because it's so much like natural language. It doesn't have too many surprises or confusing requirements. As a result, even beginning programmers find it's easy to get started coding in this language.

FLEXIBLE CODING

Ruby is very flexible, which means that there can be more than one way to code something. Programmers have more than one option and can decide which way works best for their particular project. It's because of this flexibility that some people say that they can write their Ruby code almost the same way they would speak it.

That being said, Ruby's not necessarily a simple language. It is often called dynamic, which means it operates at an exceptionally high level. Changes can be made to a Ruby program while it's running; users can modify important features in the language even while Ruby is in action. This is a process in computer programming known as reflection. This isn't a feature all Ruby programmers use, but it's a pretty cool thing to be able to do if they want to.

Another benefit of Ruby is that it can be used almost anywhere. In other words, it's portable. Ruby was developed on the GNU/Linux operating system. These days, it is used on all kinds of operating systems, such as UNIX, Mac OS X, and Windows.

NATURAL CODING

Computers need language to communicate, just like we do, but they communicate in a different way than people do. They don't understand nuance or ambiguity. Computers need a language that is logical and has a well-defined syntax. There should be a logical clarity in any instructions to a computer.

Although there are hundreds of programming languages, Ruby is popular because users think it's such a natural-feeling language. At the same time, Ruby is clear and straightforward enough for the computer. Everyone is happy!

It's important for computer language to have clarity because everything in programming is a command, or instruction, to

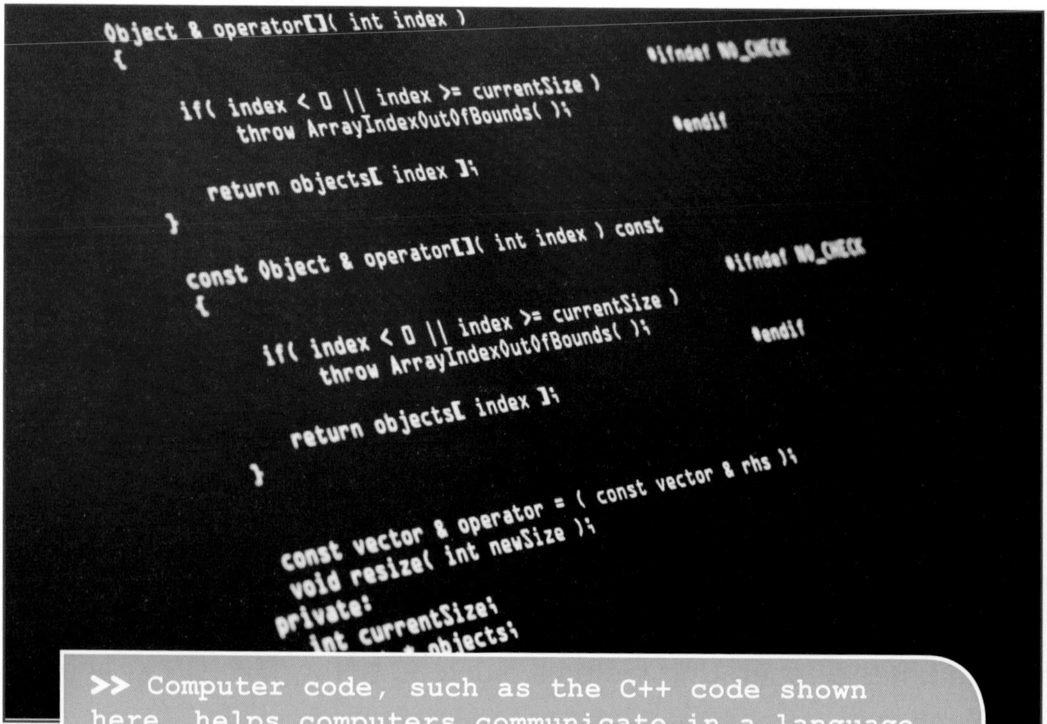

```
Object & operator[]( int index )
{
                                              #ifndef NO_CHECK
    if( index < 0 || index >= currentSize )
        throw ArrayIndexOutOfBounds( );       #endif

    return objects[ index ];
}

const Object & operator[]( int index ) const
{                                             #ifndef NO_CHECK
    if( index < 0 || index >= currentSize )
        throw ArrayIndexOutOfBounds( );       #endif

    return objects[ index ];
}

const vector & operator = ( const vector & rhs );
void resize( int newSize );
private:
    int currentSize;
        objects;
```

>> Computer code, such as the C++ code shown here, helps computers communicate in a language they understand. Users love the natural feel of Ruby's code.

the computer. Programs are built on commands and instructions, so the programmer has to be clear and specific when he or she tells the computer what to do. And because hundreds of instructions may be connected to one another to form programs, one tiny mistake can cause all kinds of problems. Uncomplicated language also helps other programmers work on and understand a program.

POWERFUL CODING

Ruby is also a powerful language. Some of its power comes from its standard library, which boasts more than nine thousand methods one can use in code. Plus, there are Ruby gems, which are like tiny libraries of code in their own right. The code in Ruby Gem software packages provides a lot more options for users. Sometimes a difficult problem that would ordinarily require an elaborate solution can be dealt with by using a gem that someone else has written. It may be just a matter of a few keystrokes to find and use a gem someone else has already written.

One handy feature of object-oriented programming is that more than one team of developers can work on the same project. An object-oriented language also makes managing the code easier for the developer.

CLEAN CODING

Ruby is well known for being a clean language. It doesn't have a lot of extra bells and whistles. It's obvious as soon as you look at Ruby that it's different. It uses English language and, unlike many other computer languages, it uses little

>> Students at Massachusetts's Winchester High School gather to examine code during an AP computer science class. Multiple users can work on projects using object-oriented platforms such as Ruby.

punctuation. This is called clean syntax. Ruby is easy to read and fairly easy to write.

Ruby can actually feel a lot like English. For example, some code that tells the computer to print "Hello World!" ten times reads like this:

```
10.times do print "Hello World!" end
```

This code might not flow as smoothly as English, but it's still quite clear what it's telling the computer to do.

>> WHEN RUBY DOESN'T GLITTER

Just because Ruby is a clean, neat language doesn't mean that users can code any old thing and have it work out. This is true of any object-oriented language, not just Ruby. Using object-oriented language doesn't mean that it will make anything a user puts into it clean and simple. It is still possible to end up with sloppy, busy code that is hard to use. Still, unlike traditional languages such as C++, Ruby and other object-oriented languages make the programming process feel so natural that complicated code isn't necessary to save time and work.

Another issue some people have with object-oriented programming is that when an error comes about, it can be very difficult to pinpoint where it occurred. To figure it out, a user has to scour every object and class to find the source of the problem. It can be time-consuming or impossible to solve the mystery in some cases.

Finally, although Ruby may be a somewhat practical programming language, some people find it difficult to master. Although users can get right to work on simple projects, some programmers find that the learning curve is pretty big.

HOW TO GET RUBY

Happily, there are several different ways for a programmer to get his or her hands on a copy of Ruby. Many software developers choose a way that has been used for years, which is called compiling software from source. For years, this has been the standard way to get open-source software, and it is actually fairly simple. One might need to download a compiler first, and then get the source code. After that, it's three easy steps and commands: configure, make, and make install. This method is best for anyone who is comfortable with the platform and wants certain settings. The third-party tools discussed next can be handy if running into problems.

Ruby newbies might have better luck with a third-party tool to install it. That being said, more advanced users can use them if they want to run more than one version of Ruby on the same computer at once. Third-party sites are not necessarily supported by Ruby, but they do have helpful communities.

Last, there's an option called the package management system. Anyone who uses a single operating system for everything he or she does may be familiar with this. Package management systems keep all the files for the programs, data, documentation, and configuration information in one place, or package. This makes them easy to move around. Better yet, the package includes knowledge, which tells it what it needs to install or even uninstall itself. People who cannot compile Ruby on their own and don't want to use a third-party tool often go with the package management system. Programmers need to make sure they are using the right package for their version of Ruby because some of them are made for older versions.

READY TO RUBY

If Ruby seems like something worth trying out, wait no longer. All it takes is an Internet connection and a computer. Kids

Ruby
A PROGRAMMER'S BEST FRIEND

Google™ Custom Search | Search |

Downloads   Documentation   Libraries   Community   News   Security   About Ruby

Download Ruby

Here you can get the latest Ruby distributions in your favorite flavor. The current stable version is 2.0.0-p353. Please be sure to read Ruby's License.

Three Ways of Installing Ruby

You can get a copy of Ruby in a variety of ways, and different people prefer each of the three methods for different reasons. Each will have a section below, but here's an overview:

- **Compiling from Source** is the standard way that software has been delivered for many, many years. This will be most familiar to the largest number of software developers.
- There are a few **third-party tools** to install Ruby. These are often simpler for total newbies or the most advanced of users.
- Finally, a few **package management systems** support Ruby. This will be most familiar to people who use one operating system for everything, and like to stick to those individual standards.

Finally, if you want to run multiple versions of Ruby on the same machine, check the **third party tools** section and use RVM. It's by far the best way to accomplish that, unless you know exactly what you're doing.

Compiling Ruby — Source code

Installing from the source code is a great solution for when you are comfortable enough with your platform and perhaps need specific settings for your environment. It's also a good solution in the event that there are no other premade packages for your platform.

If you have an issue compiling Ruby, consider using one of the third party tools in the next section. They may help you.

- Ruby 2.0.0-p353 (md5: 78282433fb697dd3613613ff55d734c1) Stable
- Ruby 1.9.3-p484 (md5: 8ac0dee72fe12d75c8b2d0ef5d0c2968) Previous
- Stable Snapshot This is a tarball of the latest snapshot of the Stable branch (ruby_2_0_0).
- Nightly Snapshot This is a tarball of whatever is in SVN, made nightly. This may contain bugs or other issues, use at your own risk!

For information about the Ruby Subversion and Git repositories, see our Ruby Core page.

Get Started, it's easy!

Try Ruby! (in your browser)
Ruby in Twenty Minutes
Ruby from Other Languages

Explore a new world...

Documentation
Books
Libraries
Success Stories

Participate in a friendly and growing community.

Mailing Lists: **Talk about Ruby with programmers from all around the world.**

User Groups: **Get in contact with Rubyists in your area.**

Weblogs: **Read about what's happening right now in the Ruby community.**

Ruby Core: **Help polish the rough edges of the latest Ruby.**

Issue Tracking: **Report or help solve issues in Ruby.**

Some Top Ruby Projects

More...

Syndicate

Recent News (RSS)

>> These instructions from the Ruby website give compiling instructions. There are several different ways that users can download Ruby software onto their computers.

Ruby at http://kidsruby.com teaches kids, or anyone, how to start using Ruby. The Kids Ruby site even offers a sneak peak of what Ruby looks like and how it works before anything is downloaded. It doesn't take long to start writing code and see how the language works. Keep with it, and the lessons get more involved. Kids Ruby is free and works on any kind of computer. Adults or older kids who don't care for the graphics of Kids Ruby can click their way over to Code School's TryRuby at http://tryruby.org. It just takes a few minutes to try out the tutorial and start using code right on the screen without installing a thing. Just follow the directions on the screen and get ready to see Ruby in action.

THE NOT-SO-SURPRISING HISTORY OF RUBY

Yukihiro Matsumoto taught himself how to program computers. Later, he went on to graduate from college with a degree in information science. Matsumoto started developing what would become Ruby in 1993. He loved the power of scripting languages and felt like they had a lot of potential. He also thought that they would work well with object-oriented programming.

>> Yukihiro Matsumoto, the founder of Ruby, speaks at the annual Ruby conference, EuRuKo, in 2011.

PICKING AND CHOOSING

Looking around the Internet, Matsumoto didn't find quite what he sought. He was in search of a language that was more powerful than Perl and more object-oriented than Python. He wanted to create a natural language, but not one that was too simple. So he decided to pick and choose what he liked most about Perl, Smalltalk, Eiffel, Ada, and Lisp. He mixed these characteristics together to create Ruby.

What Matsumoto liked about Perl was its power to do things more than one way because everyone is different. What works for one person may not work for another. Here's where Ruby differs from Python, explains Matsumoto. Python may be considered more readable, but it offers only one way to do things. With Ruby, users can find their own way of doing things.

And Ruby's design is made for humans. It takes the pressure of programming off the programmer and places it squarely on the computer. The computer does more work, so the user can get more done. All this occurs with smaller but more readable code.

READY, SET, RUBY! RUBY RELEASES

Ruby's alpha version came out in 1994. Ruby 0.95 was released in 1995: three later versions were released in the next two days. Matsumoto worked all on his own until 1996. After that, a Ruby community formed. Although he still does most of his work alone, the Ruby community works together to add repairs and patches. Ruby is constantly changing and improving.

>> RUBY FOR FREE!

It's true. Anyone can download and use Ruby for free. This is because Ruby is an open-source programming language. Users can use, copy, change, and share their Ruby code. In fact, sharing and changing and copying are all encouraged!

Open-source software is nothing new. It has been around since the 1980s and started to get really popular ten years later when the Internet became all the rage. Open-source software and hardware allows users to develop and improve the product, then share what they've done with others. An open-source approach means the coding can be used to educate. Every new code is a new creation for the Ruby community. Another benefit to open-source sharing is that things are always changing, growing, and developing. This type of sharing promotes creativity.

Ruby takes advantage of its ever-growing and more diverse community of users and developers all over the world. They constantly improve, update, and maintain Ruby. RubyTalk is just one of several Ruby mailing lists. On RubyTalk, users can learn about Ruby basics. Ruby Forum is an online forum where anyone can ask other users questions and get advice.

In 1995, within the first few days of the release of Ruby 0.95 to Japanese newsgroups, a mailing list formed that is still lively to this day. It wasn't until 1999 that English-speaking countries started to catch on to Ruby. RubyTalk was the first English-language mailing list. Newsgroups and online forums also popped up everywhere as places where people could learn about and discuss Ruby. This is a huge benefit of Ruby. There may only be a few people developing Ruby, but its community is constantly growing and helping advance Ruby.

It wasn't until 2005, when Ruby on Rails made its debut, that the Ruby language really made an unforgettable splash on the programming scene. Ruby on Rails is a Web-based application framework that is written in Ruby and only Ruby. The same year, Apple included Rails with its Mac OS X operating system, called Leopard, and Ruby on Rails became even more popular.

In the fall of 2013, Ruby released a preview of its newest version: Ruby 2.1.0–preview1. It gave users an early glance at the newest features of Ruby 2.1.

THE JOY OF PROGRAMMING

In an interview with Bill Venners for Artima.com, Matsumoto wrote, "For me the purpose of life is partly to have joy. Programmers often feel joy when they can concentrate on the creative side of programming, so Ruby is designed to make programmers happy." If this seems like an odd approach to programming, Matsumoto disagrees. People are happier, he theorizes, when they can concentrate on the work at hand, getting it done quickly and enjoying it along the way. When he created Ruby, he set out to come up with a language that is neat and crisp. Ruby is not weighed down by a lot of extras to distract users from being productive. And, if all goes according to plan, they have a good time doing it.

This is where the "principle of least surprise" comes in. Whether or not Matsumoto coined the term (there are stories on

>> Ruby was created so that users could have fun with programming, not experience frustration or do more work than was necessary.

the Internet saying he did and still others where he denies it), it fits. He wanted to program without being exasperated while at the same time not doing more work than he had to. In short, he wanted programming to be a whole lot of fun. The principle of least surprise is sometimes misunderstood, though. It doesn't mean that using Ruby means programmers will never be faced with problems or unexpected issues. Matsumoto created a language that doesn't surprise him. And he feels the term doesn't apply to Ruby until one knows it inside and out. He points out that even after programming in C++ for two or three years, he was still surprised.

THE NAME GAME

Once he came up with the language he wanted, Matsumoto realized he had to come up with a name for it. He brainstormed in an online chat with his friend Keiju Ishitsuka for possible ideas, joking that it should be named after a gemstone, to follow in the footsteps of Perl. Keiju Ishitsuka suggested Ruby, and he also considered the word "coral" for the language. Matsumoto finally decided on Ruby in part because it was the birthstone of one of his coworkers. His other reason for choosing Ruby was because the gemstone is known for its bright red sparkle and great value.

MORE THAN RUBY, MORE THAN ONE

Although Matsumoto might be best known for his work with Ruby, he's also one of Japan's biggest fans of open source. He has worked for a Japanese open-source company called Netlab.jp. And Ruby isn't his only open-source project; it's just the first one to become well known beyond Japan's borders. He has also released Cmail, which is a mail user manager.

Matsumoto also tells programmers that they should learn more than just one language and more than just one style. His logic is that every language and system has its own cultures. Knowing many programming languages and systems exposes the user to the programming culture's ideas and gives her or him a more expansive point of view. Ruby was developed using several different programming languages, so maybe it's no surprise that Matz thinks this way.

Matsumoto read a lot of different codes to learn how to be a better programmer. He says that reading about coding in textbooks is great, but reading actual code is better still—and he argues that reading code is even better than writing it. Reading code helps programmers become better at their work. This

```
import java.io.*;
import java.util.Date;

public class SaveDate {

    public static void main(String args[])
        FileOutputStream fos = new Fi
        ObjectOutputStream oos = new O
        Date date = new Date();
        oos.writeObject(date);
        oos.flush();
        oos.close();
        fos.close();
```

>> Matsumoto encourages programmers to read as much code as possible when they are learning so that they can understand the ins and outs of the code.

approach helps one understand the programmer's views and feelings. Reading code teaches one what the programmer was trying to do and how he or she did it. If a user is trying to do something in particular with code, says Matsumoto, reading code and then trying it out can be a quick and easy learning tool. Seeing the code work out an algorithm by running a debugger can be extremely educational.

Matsumoto doesn't think any one programming language—not even Ruby—should be able to do everything. He didn't even try to make Ruby a perfect language because what is ideal for one person isn't necessarily perfect for everybody. Instead of focusing on what it does, when he created Ruby he thought about how it made him feel while he was using it: happy.

PUTTING RUBY TO WORK

Anyone who is already interested in Ruby might be thinking ahead and wondering if knowing how to work with Ruby or Ruby on Rails can result in a job or even a career. It sure can! A background in Ruby or Ruby on Rails is a great job skill to have, whether it's learned in college or if one teaches himself or herself. Ruby is cutting edge and creative, so it can be used to build some cool web applications. Think of Hulu, Basecamp, and Campfire: all of those were built with Ruby on Rails. And that, in turn, might result in a nice paycheck. If that sounds good, check out some jobs that list Ruby or Rails as a main skill.

It's well known that both Ruby and Ruby on Rails are easy to learn, so just about anyone can do it. Programmers can teach themselves through practice, books, and tutorials. And don't forget the strong online community with its wealth of information. That's another tremendous source of knowledge and a great place to go when one has questions about figuring out a tricky bit of code or another problem.

Though Ruby developers can learn on their own, others learn Ruby by taking some night classes while doing other work. Still others opt to go to college full-time for programming and learn all about Ruby and Ruby on Rails there, along with plenty of other computer coding and programming skills.

Ruby programmers can work from home right out of college or get a job working for a company. Working from home doesn't

>> Ruby can be learned in the classroom by attending college full-time or doing it gradually, such as through night classes. Some people take the initiative to learn it on their own.

have to mean freelancing, constantly looking for the next job or contract. With the increasing popularity of telecommuting, it may be possible to get a full-time job working for a business or company and work from home most days and just go into the office a couple of days a week. Others allow employees to work from home full-time. There's a job style out there for almost any Ruby programmer.

Those eager to work on Ruby on Rails will not be disappointed. Big companies such as VMware, Salesforce, and HP are using Ruby, so there may very well be increasing demand for Rails developers. Tom Mornini declares on BusinessInsider.com, "In fact, it's nearly impossible to be an unemployed Ruby on Rails developer."

CHAPTER 3

RUBY SHINES: PROGRAMMING IN ACTION

Once Ruby is up and running, there are lots of ways to have more fun with it by making it do more, run faster, or do almost anything the programmer wants. Until 2006, the only dependable way to run Ruby scripts was to use the official Ruby implementation MRI (Matz's Ruby Interpreter) that Matsumoto and his team developed. Now there are lots of implementations out there. Some of the more popular include JRuby and IronRuby.

JRUBY

The open-source implementation known as JRuby runs on the JVM, or Java Virtual Machine. JRuby opens up a wealth of Java options: libraries, distribution tools, and application servers. Java fans can write in Ruby code but then use Java when they need it. It helps them avoid an awkward stack of different elements or what author and software developer Zed Shaw calls a "Frankenstack." Some feel that JRuby is the strongest alternative to running the MRI. It's considered fast and a good performer for using every day, especially in situations where Java is already

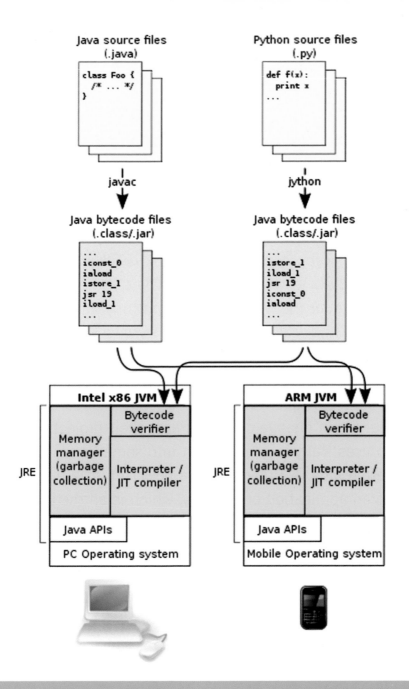

>> By using the Java Virtual Machine, shown here, JRuby users can write in Ruby and access Java—and thus a wider range of options—whenever they want.

in use. And JRuby is simple to install: Just download it, unpack it, and run it. It's ready to go.

IRONRUBY

IronRuby is the alternative implementation for Microsoft users, specifically the .NET platform, where applications are built in Microsoft. Microsoft's own John Lam is the lead developer of the open-source IronRuby. "Iron" stands for "implementation running on .NET." It works as a dependable option for anyone who wants to run Ruby code right on the .NET common language runtime, or CLR. It's flexible in that it lets the user choose the right language for the work at hand. IronRuby runs on Windows, UNIX, Linux, and Mac, just to name a few.

GEMS MAKE RUBY SPARKLE!

Programmers can use Ruby and the Ruby Standard Library to play around and change code to create their projects. But anyone who uses Ruby is going to run into some handy little Ruby gems before long. A Ruby gem is a powerful little package that contains an application or a library, which is all the information and data needed to be installed on a system. Each gem is different, but all have the same basic structure that includes a name, version number, and description.

The big deal about gems is that when a programmer runs into a problem or wants to add something specific, there might already be a gem out there that does so. Someone else may have already come across this problem or wanted to make the same sort of change and created a gem for it.

Gems can save a lot of time and frustration. If someone finds a gem that doesn't do quite what he or she wants, it's no problem. Gems (and Ruby, of course) are flexible and can be tweaked or improved to do something different or do more. Another reason why people like Ruby gems is because they have a lot more options than a basic Ruby library.

FORKING

Maybe there's a gem out there that does something close to what a project needs, but not quite. That gem can be adapted or improved in a process known as forking. Think of it in terms of actual silverware, where an extra tine is added to a fork. The fork still operates as it was intended, but now it does the job in a different, possibly even better, way with the extra tine.

Ruby forking is when someone takes an open-source gem (or other application) and improves on it. Then he or she reposts it, according to the open-source guidelines. Forking is taking the application in a slightly new direction, making improvements and other changes so that the gem can accomplish something a little different or a little better.

GISTS

Sometimes a programmer wants something even simpler than a gem, though. Gists are bits of code that are copied and shared. Gists are smaller than gems, usually consisting of only a few lines of code. Creating a gist is almost as easy as copying and pasting in a word processing document. The web-based hosting service GitHub launched Gist in 2008.

>> >> GET GOING TO GITHUB

GitHub is considered a pretty special site because it's a site where people can share and publish code, but it's also a kind of programmers' social networking site. GitHub was an open-source project started by Linus Torvalds, who also created the operating system called Linux. At the center of GitHub is Git, which is responsible for handling and monitoring project revisions. GitHub has a trifecta of features: fork, pull request, and merge.

Before GitHub, it was a huge hassle with many steps before one could contribute to an open-source project. Now, GitHub allows users to fork a project. Then, using a pull request, users can post their changes to the project for others, including the person maintaining the original project, to see and review. Also visible are the pull requester's profile and all the projects that person has contributed to. If the pull is accepted, the requester gets credit on the original site and this contribution shows up along with his or her other contributions. GitHub also provides a place for users to talk about different patches.

RUBYGEMS

RubyGems is a system for managing those little packages called gems. In other words, it's a way to collect, install, and distribute libraries of related code. Developers can manage their gems and easily install them, even different versions of the same libraries. Other languages like Perl have similar abilities. One major Ruby gem is called Ruby on Rails.

SING IT, SINATRA!

One popular Ruby gem is called Sinatra, a small domain-specific language (DSL) that makes creating web applications in Ruby a snap. Sinatra is a kind of library that helps the user handle http from the server side. It handles requests and responses from a server.

Sinatra allows users to build an app easily. All someone needs to get started is Sinatra and a few gems. Sinatra is considered very stable because its framework stays basically the same. Users have a lot of control with Sinatra, although programmers might have to put more time and thought into their application.

>> Websites such as the BBC's run using the Ruby gem known as Sinatra, which is well-known for being stable but flexible.

And if there's a problem, Sinatra isn't much help in solving it. A lot of valuable time can be eaten up trying to figure out solutions to bugs and other problems. Sinatra is also known for its complete lack of conventions. That means it's extremely flexible.

Blake Mizerany created Sinatra in 2007, and as of late 2013, it had been downloaded more than nine million times from the website RubyGems.org. Sites such as Apple, GitHub, and the BBC all run using Sinatra.

COME OUT OF YOUR SHELL

Ruby comes with a handy tool written by Keiju Ishitsuka called Interactive Ruby (IRB), which helps users experiment. The IRB comes already installed right along with Ruby, so there's a shell in place where one can try things out. The Ruby shell works in a similar way as an operating system shell and provides a way for the user to communicate with the operating system—or in this case, the IRB.

Users can simply type "irb" at the beginning of a command and start typing a command. Results appear right away, so users can immediately see what would happen without having to write an entire program. Done using IRB? Just type "exit" or "quit" to exit. Many users prefer using IRB to play around with Ruby and see how things work.

RAILING ON RUBY

For all of Ruby's programming strengths, however, there are a number of operational limitations and drawbacks as well. For instance, some users have found that using the original Ruby, or

Matz's Ruby Interpreter (MRI), which is almost entirely written in C, uses way too much C for their tastes. Some say it's just as likely that the MRI will make a project ridiculously difficult as it will make it easy.

Ruby isn't recommended if there's a lot of data to handle. Unfortunately, using Ruby to handle a large upload brings to light lots of bugs that cause plenty of issues. Image manipulation can get particularly messy because the main libraries the language uses are slow and can take an extremely long time to install on most systems.

Other languages are a lot better at math than Ruby as well. If the job requires a lot of computation, Ruby users have to

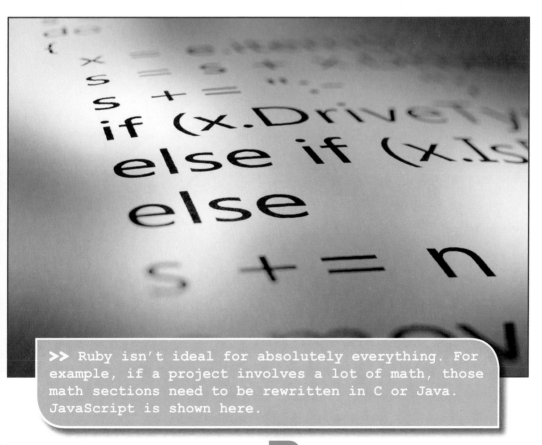

>> Ruby isn't ideal for absolutely everything. For example, if a project involves a lot of math, those math sections need to be rewritten in C or Java. JavaScript is shown here.

rewrite the sections related to math in C or Java. Then, when a new version of Ruby comes out, these parts have to be written all over again. Ruby may be fine for most applications, but if scientific or financial calculations are necessary, perhaps it's not the best choice.

Another complaint some Ruby users have is that errors can be bewildering. Ruby can build some spiffy domain-specific languages (DSL), but when an error occurs with the DSL, it shows up as a Ruby error. That can be very frustrating when trying to get to the bottom of a problem.

Finally, e-mail processing is another weak point for Ruby. Python, Perl, C#, C++, Java, and C have all been said to have

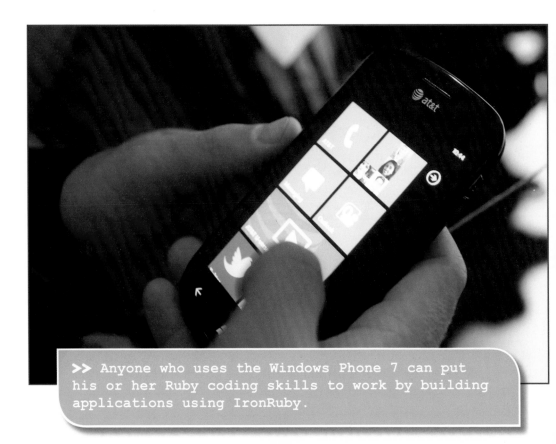

>> Anyone who uses the Windows Phone 7 can put his or her Ruby coding skills to work by building applications using IronRuby.

better e-mail options. While it's possible for Ruby to process e-mail, the system can be slow and have strange bugs.

RUBY PROJECTS: MORE THAN WEBSITES

Ruby is known far and wide for being a tool to help build websites. But there are plenty of other uses for Ruby, too. For example, it's easy to make a cool computer game using Ruby and a gem called Gosu. Fans of the falling block game *Tetris* can create a game aptly named *Falling Blocks*. If Sudoku is more your style, Ruby can help with that, too. On the more serious side, Ruby can be used to build a conversion calculator or an income tax calculator. Apps for the Windows Phone 7 run on Iron Ruby.

RubyMotion is also used to create apps. RubyMotion runs on the Mac operating systems iOs and OSx. For example, RubyMotion is used in the app ShakeShare: Shareable Shakespeare. Need a Shakespearean quote or joke? Just shake your device and a new quote comes up. Let's Camp helps plan next weekend's camping trip. Album Alert works with Facebook to help keep track of new releases.

CHAPTER 4

TAKING A RIDE ON THE RAILS

Anyone who is already hooked on Ruby as a way to build web applications has undoubtedly heard about Ruby on Rails, or Rails, as it is often nicknamed. Rails takes the strength and flexibility of the Ruby programming language and puts it in a framework that does a whole lot of work to help developers.

RAILS ON THE RIGHT TRACK

In 2003, a software developer named David Heinemeier Hansson created Ruby on Rails for "programmer happiness and beautiful code," as he describes on his website at http://David.HeinemeierHansson.com. Rails first entered the world through a web-application company called 37Signals, where Hansson was a partner. Using the company's product, called Basecamp, as a jumping-off point, Hansson created Ruby on Rails for use within 37Signals only. However, Hansson and the company soon realized that their internal product could

>> David Heinemeier Hansson created Ruby on Rails for private use but soon realized that the program would appeal to everyone. The framework was released to the general public in 2004.

be put to good use by the general public. Ruby on Rails was released in 2004.

Version 1 followed at the end of 2005. In 2007, Ruby on Rails really started to get people's attention when Apple started selling it as part of its Mac OS X operating system Leopard. Several more upgrades were issued; as of 2013, the latest iteration was Ruby on Rails 4.

RUBY'S BEEN FRAMED!

Ruby on Rails is a web application framework that uses the Ruby programming language. Like Ruby, it is an open-source product. Ruby on Rails is written in Ruby language and runs right within Ruby. It's a library of software that gives the Ruby language the ability to do even more.

Ruby on Rails is a frame for creating websites. It takes the Ruby language and combines it with HTML, CSS, and JavaScript. Together, they create a web application. This Web application runs on a server, which makes Rails a server-side or back-end development platform, and the web browser is the "front end."

BETTER AND FASTER ON RAILS

Ruby on Rails makes it easy for the developer to work quickly and in the end have hearty and vigorous applications. Rails simplifies the process of working with databases and objects, but the developer doesn't have to put a ridiculous amount of time into the planning process. It can be a possible solution to the frustration of managing everything that goes into writing web applications.

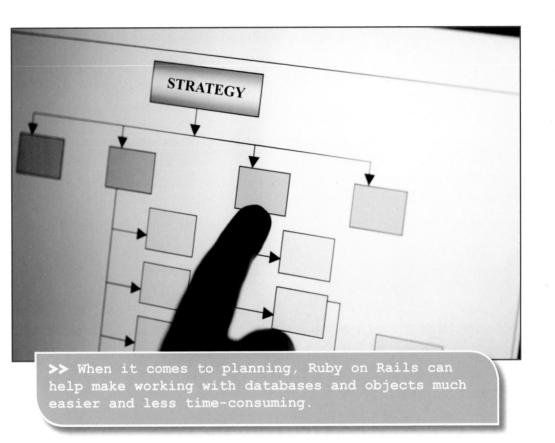

>> When it comes to planning, Ruby on Rails can help make working with databases and objects much easier and less time-consuming.

Programmers who already know other languages may find that Ruby on Rails code looks fairly familiar. That being said, the code might not be used in exactly the same way. Ruby programmers have used it a bit differently.

Getting to work with Rails does involve figuring out some complex skills, but they're far from unbeatable. And depending on what kind of applications the user has in mind, it may not be necessary to dive into the most complex parts of Rails unless he or she wants to. Even users who don't consider themselves Ruby programming experts can start out with a fairly simple

>> RUBY ON RAILS AND THE THREE RULES

Even though Ruby on Rails is constantly changing and improving, it sticks to three basic principles. First and foremost, Ruby on Rails always uses Ruby as its programming language.

Second, it consistently uses the same architecture, or structure. Embedded in the structure of Rails is a special pattern that is called a Model-View-Controller (MVC). Although MVC might seem a little abstract, it's a very common pattern and worth knowing. The model stands for knowledge, which can be one single object or a group of them. The view is a visual representation of the model. A controller links the user to the system. MVC makes code maintenance easier, too.

Finally (and maybe most important, according to Hansson), the programmer has to be happy. Rails makes Rubyists happy by making it easy to be productive. In no time at all they can create a web application with pages and templates and more.

application or make use of Ruby's more advanced features without knowing every last detail.

Ruby on Rails can pack a whole lot of punch. Sure, it offers plenty of power, but not everyone really needs all that. Don't be discouraged: with Rails 3x, it's possible to build even a very small application.

>> No matter what programming language coders use, they must decide how much they want to work within the language's conventions and infrastructure and how much they want to build their own framework in order to achieve their desired outcome.

FOLLOWING THE GOLDEN PATH

Ruby on Rails is well known for focusing on "convention over configuration," writes Sayanee Basu on Net.tutsplus.com. In other words, Rails users generally do their best work if they follow Rails rules instead of trying to configure, or build, their own framework. This is why so many relish Rails. In Rails, the programmer needs to code only the parts of the program that are not standard. Ruby on Rails "comes with its own tools and settings," but the programmer is certainly under no obligation to use them.

Apps can be configured in whatever way the developer wants, even though sticking to the Rails conventions are recommended. In an interview with Edd Dumbill for the O'Reilly Network website, the creator, Hannsson, pointed out, "With Rails, you trade flexibility at the infrastructure level to gain flexibility at the application level. If you are happy to work along the golden path that I've embedded in Rails, you gain an immense reward in terms of productivity that allows you to do more, sooner, and better at the application level."

By following those Rails conventions, or rules, the programmer doesn't need to spend as much time making decisions because a lot of what he or she needs is already there. This makes it easier to work faster, cooperate better, and be more efficient with maintenance. As Daren Jones comments on his website, SitePoint.com, "Rails is involved and large because it contains solutions to most of the problems that most people building apps of such scale will encounter. Trying to recreate all these solutions by hand is the anti-simplicity. The default Rails app provides a lot that I need which requires extra setup in Sinatra. This can lead to faster development in Rails."

KEEPING IT REAL WITH ASD

In the wild, wide world of software application development there lurks a method called agile software development (ASD). ASD is basically just a flexible way of managing the creative process while being pragmatic, or realistic. It keeps code simple, encourages lots of testing, and offers up useful pieces of the application whenever they're ready, which means not

>> THREE, TWO, ONE, SCRUM!

Agile software development has one model, or framework, called Scrum. In rugby, a scrum, or scrummage, refers to a formation that restarts the game after it has been stopped for some reason. In the coding world, Scrum is made up of many small groups working together in a concentrated effort.

The group leader is sort of like a project manager but is better known as a ScrumMaster. Scrum teams have to be great communicators, manage themselves well, and be able to make good decisions. One of the main principles of Scrum is that unexpected project changes, sometimes called requirements churn, will come up but can be made quickly, even though the solution may not be handled in a traditional way. It's all about being flexible, fast, and creative.

waiting to unveil a huge project until it is completely finished. Bits and pieces are created and shared as the project progresses.

The focus of Ruby on Rails on convention over configuration and software testing makes it an ideal match for ASD. Ruby on Rails is able to deal with change, which can be a miserable process. However, Rails uses migrations, so it can switch from one database to another without tears. By using migration objects, which are all individually time stamped and organized, if something goes wrong with the migration, the whole shebang can just be rolled back to a previous stable version. Migration objects also make it easier to fix a bug when it comes up.

RAPID PROTOTYPING WITH RAILS

Rapid prototyping is used when one needs to quickly create models, or prototypes. With rapid prototyping, one can make a visual. They say a picture is worth a thousand words, right? By using rapid prototyping, a model is available to show others. Users make a mock-up of a project, whether it's a website, an application, or whatever. Once there's a model, the creator can share it with others for feedback and make improvements. There are all kinds of rapid prototyping techniques. They can be anything from a basic sketch on paper with pencil to well-developed creations that practically look and perform like a final product.

Rails jumps in with lots of gems to help make rapid prototyping go even faster and smoother. For example, Active Admin helps create an administration panel that is extremely useful and looks pretty snazzy, too. Basic forms are easy as pie with Ruby on Rails, but using a gem like Formtastic or SimpleForm can make them look and perform better. Resque Mailer saves time when it comes to sending out e-mails. Testing is an important part of any project, whether it's in rapid prototyping or not. Cucumber and RSpec are two gems that help make that testing phase more efficient. After the testing phase, it's time to put the code into action. Plenty of people like Rails hosts such as Heroku and Engine Yard, but gems including Phusion Passenger or Capistrano might be thriftier choices.

LESS RISK, MORE DATA

Custom software can sometimes be pricey, and some of the packaged software options result in a website that looks a lot like every other website. That's not such a great feature when a company is looking to stand out and make a statement. Rails makes it possible for a company's IT (information technology) department to get new projects moving quickly without risking a huge cost if the new app it wants to build is uncertain at all.

Additionally, Ruby is sturdy enough to handle sites that attract hundreds of millions of users, whereas some of its

>> If a company isn't 100 percent sure its app is going to work, Ruby on Rails lets the company's IT department start building without spending a lot.

competitors can only manage hundreds of thousands at most. Even if Ruby on Rails doesn't seem like exactly the right fit for a web development project, check out the Rails community.

RAILING ON RAILS: TOO MUCH MAGIC?

As popular as Ruby on Rails has become, naturally not everyone loves it. Sure, it has a massive library, but some people find that the Ruby on Rails library reference is almost too big. Such a large library can make finding what one is searching for difficult and time-consuming.

Some programmers love that Ruby on Rails is constantly changing and improving, but for others this can be a frustration. It can be really annoying to finally master one aspect of Rails only to find out that it's been changed.

Rails works better for web applications than it does for web servers. Rails has a lot of rules and conventions, so if a programmer wants to do something beyond the Rails conventions, he or she may be out of luck.

If a project has been using Ruby on Rails for a long time, maybe even years, the code can become very messy. In a way, some programmers think this says a lot about the Rails platform. Users can keep adding to it until it works without wasting a lot of time testing and reloading. In other programs, this can take a long time. "Ruby on Rails has an impressively low barrier to fiddling," says Avdi Grimm on his *Virtuous Code* blog. The problem comes up when Rails reaches what he calls a "productivity crash." All that tinkering and the shortcuts build up until little changes that used to take no time at all start to take weeks.

The ease of using Rails might also be its undoing. It's so effortless to get started using Ruby on Rails that some programmers complain that there is lots of focus on how easy it is but not as much focus on doing it well. In contrast, the Perl community emphasizes the importance of high-quality programming.

RAILS RUNS EVERYWHERE

Whatever issues some may have with Rails, that hasn't stopped many companies—from large corporations to small, part-time operations—from using the framework to get ahead in business.

>> The next time you catch up on your favorite TV show on Hulu, remember it was built using Ruby on Rails from the beginning.

More than two hundred thousand websites are humming along thanks to the power of Ruby on Rails. Some of these sites are used all the time: Amazon, Yahoo!, and CNET all use Ruby in one way or another. Even the National Aeronautics and Space Administration (NASA) uses Ruby on Rails.

The original Ruby on Rails app was, of course, 37signals's Basecamp. From there it has gone on to be instrumental in running high-profile, high-traffic sites like Shopify and Best Buy. People who enjoy streaming and catching up on their favorite television shows on Hulu can thank Ruby on Rails, too. Even the gem site GitHub runs on Rails.

Ruby and Ruby on Rails have come barreling down the track with a whole lot of steam over the past several years. As more people find out about them and take advantage of the simple, open-source programming, the more popular they may become. And it looks like they're only going to keep picking up more speed.

ALGORITHM   A group of rules or processes followed in calculations or other problem-solving tasks, often by a computer.

ALPHA The first in a series.

COMMON LANGUAGE RUNTIME (CLR) Runs code and
helps make developing simpler.

DEBUG To find and repair errors and mistakes ("bugs") in
computer hardware or software.

DOMAIN SPECIFIC LANGUAGE (DSL) A language
designed to work on a specific problem in a specific space.

FORUM A place where people can share their views and ideas.

FRAMEWORK A software framework that supports the development of Web applications.

IMPLEMENTATION An object or tool used to execute a task.

ITERATION A new version of computer hardware or
software.

JAVA A general computer programming language to help programs run on any computer system.

LIBRARY   A group of helpful data for shared use.

METHOD A piece of code that achieves a job.

.NET PLATFORM   Pronounced "dot net," a Microsoft framework for building applications.

PLATFORM   A standard way of operating around which software can be developed.

PROGRAMMING   The process of creating and running a set of
instructions that make a computer perform certain tasks
and functions.

REFLECTION   Ruby's ability to analyze itself.

SCRIPTING A series of instructions carried out automatically and in a certain order.

SHELL The outermost layer of a computer operating system; short for shell program, it offers a border between the user and the operating system.

STACK A group of locations for storing data so that the most recent is the first to be recovered.

STRING CLASS An arrangement of characters, words, or other data in a line.

TELECOMMUTING Working from home using the Internet, e-mail, and the telephone.

American Computer Science League
10 Brisas Drive
West Warwick, RI 02893
E-mail: info@acsl.org
Website: http://www.acsl.org
The American Computer Science League manages contests in
computer science and computer programming for junior
and senior high school students from the United States,
Canada, Europe, and Asia.

Canadian Association of Computer Science
Department of Computer Science
University of Calgary
2500 University Drive NW
Calgary, AB T2N 1N4
Canada
Website: http://cacsaic.org
The Canadian Association of Computer Science endeavors to
heighten student interest in the study of computer science.
The organization offers news, conferences, academic job
opportunities, and more.

Ladies Learning Code
CSI Annex
720 Bathurst Street
5th Floor
Toronto, ON M5S 2R4

Canada

E-mail: info@ladieslearningcode.com

Website: http://ladieslearningcode.com

This Toronto-based not-for-profit organization runs workshops for women, men, girls, and boys who want to learn computer programming and other technical skills in a beginner-friendly environment.

Rails Girls

E-mail: team@railsgirls.com

Website: http://railsgirls.com

Rails Girls provides tools and a community for women to learn about technology and expand ideas by making building things fun and technology accessible.

The Ruby Association

Matsue Terrsa Annex 2F

478-18 Asahi-cho Matsue Shimane 690-2102

Japan

E-mail: info@ruby-assn.org

Website: http://www.ruby.or.jp

The Ruby Association was created to improve Ruby language development. It continues to support Ruby-related projects with communities and businesses.

Ruby Central

E-mail: contact@rubycentral.org

Website: http://rubycentral.org

Ruby Central, Inc. is a nonprofit organization that was founded in 2001 to support and advocate for the worldwide Ruby community. It organizes the annual conferences known as RubyConf and RailsConf where Rubyists can collaborate and network.

WEBSITES

Due to the changing nature of Internet links, Rosen Publishing has developed an online list of websites related to the subject of this book. This site is updated regularly. Please use the following link to access this list:

http://www.rosenlinks.com/CODE/Ruby

Aimonetti, Matt. *MacRuby: The Definitive Guide*. Sebastopol, CA: O'Reilly Media, 2012.

Black, David A. *The Well-grounded Rubyist: [covers Ruby 1.9.1]*. Greenwich, CT: Manning, 2009.

Brookshear, J. Glenn. *Computer Science: An Overview*. Upper Saddle River, NJ: Prentice Hall, 2011.

Carlson, Lucas, and Leonard Richardson. *Ruby Cookbook*. Sebastopol, CA: O'Reilly, 2006.

David, Flanagan, and Matsumoto Yukihiro. *The Ruby Programming Language*. Sebastopol, CA: O'Reilly, 2008.

Fernandez, Obed. *Rails 4 Way*. Upper Saddle River, NJ: Addison-Wesley, 2014.

Fitzgerald, Michael. *Learning Ruby*. Sebastopol, CA: O'Reilly, 2007.

Freedman, Jerri. *Careers in Computer Science and Programming*. New York, NY; Rosen Publishing, 2011.

Frieder, Ophir, Gideon Frieder, and David A. Grossman. *Computer Science Programming Basics in Ruby*. Sebastopol, CA: O'Reilly, 2013.

Fulton, Hal Edwin. *The Ruby Way: Solutions and Techniques in Ruby Programming*. 3rd ed. Boston, MA: Addison-Wesley, 2013.

Hardnett, Charles R. *Programming Like a Pro for Teens*. Boston, MA: Cengage Learning, 2012.

Hartl, Michael. *Ruby on Rails Tutorial: Learn Web Developments with Rails*. Upper Saddle River, NJ: Addison-Wesley, 2013.

Metz, Sandi. *Practical Object-oriented Design in Ruby: An Agile Primer*. Upper Saddle River, NJ: Addison-Wesley, 2013.

Olsen, Russ. *Eloquent Ruby.* Upper Saddle River, NJ: Addison-Wesley, 2011.

Ruby, Sam. *Agile Web Development with Rails 4.* Raleigh, NC: Pragmatic Programmers, 2013.

Sande, Warren, and Carter Sande. *Hello World! Computer Programming for Kids (and Other Beginners).* Greenwich, CT: Manning, 2013.

Thomas, David, Chad Fowler, and Andrew Hunt. *Programming Ruby 1.9 & 2.0: The Pragmatic Programmers' Guide.* Raleigh, NC: Pragmatic Bookshelf, 2013.

Wang, Wally. *Beginning Programming All-in-One Desk Reference for Dummies.* Hoboken, NJ: Wiley, 2008.

{BIBLIOGRAPHY

Basu, Sayanee. "Ruby on Rails Study Guide: The History of Rails."
     Tuts+, January 22, 2013. Retrieved October 30, 2013 (http://
     net.tutsplus.com/articles/ruby-on-rails-study-guide-the
     -history-of-rails).

Burgess, Andrew. "Ruby for Newbies: Installing and Getting
     Started." Tuts+, October 10, 2010. Retrieved October 30,
     2013 (http://net.tutsplus.com/tutorials/ruby/ruby-for
     -newbies-installing-ruby-and-getting-started).

Cooper, Peter. *Beginning Ruby: From Novice to Professional.*
     New York, NY: Apress, 2009.

Dumbill, Edd. "Interview with David Heinemeier Hansson." O'Reilly
     Media. Retrieved October 19, 2013 (http://www.oreillynet
     .com/network/2005/08/30/ruby-rails-david-heinemeier
     -hansson.html).

Finley, Klint. "What Exactly Is GitHub Anyway?" TechCrunch, July
     14, 2012. Retrieved October 30, 2013 (http://techcrunch
     .com/2012/07/14/what-exactly-is-github-anyway).

Ford, Jerry Lee. *Ruby Programming for the Absolute Beginner.*
     Boston, MA: Thomson, 2007.

Grimm, Avdi. "Your Code Is My Hell." *Virtuous Code*, August 22,
     2011. Retrieved October 17, 2013 (http://devblog.avdi.org/
     2011/08/22/your-code-is-my-hell).

Gunner Technology. "The History of Ruby." November 29, 2011.
     Retrieved October 30, 2013 (http://www.gunnertech.com/
     2011/11/the-history-of-ruby).

Hansson, David Heinemeier. Retrieved October 21, 2013 (http://
     david.heinemeierhansson.com).

Jones, Darren. "Rails or Sinatra: The Best of Both Worlds?"
SitePoint, January 16, 2012. Retrieved October 30, 2013
(http://www.sitepoint.com/rails-or-sinatra-the-best-of
-both-worlds).

Mornini, Tom. "Here's Why Ruby on Rails Is Hot." Business Insider,
May 11, 2000. Retrieved October 30, 2013 (http://www
.businessinsider.com/heres-why-ruby-on-rails-is-hot-2011-5)

Ruby. "About Ruby." Retrieved October 30, 2013 (https://
www.ruby-lang.org/en/about).

Shaw, Zed. "You Used Ruby to Write WHAT?!" March 1, 2008.
Retrieved October 27, 2013 (http://www.cio.com/article/
191000/You_Used_Ruby_to_Write_WHAT_?page=
2&taxonomyId=3038).

Silva, Goncalo. "Ruby Gems—What, Why and How." Ruby
Learning, December 14, 2010. Retrieved October 30, 2013
(http://rubylearning.com/blog/2010/12/14/ruby-gems
-%E2%80%94-what-why-and-how).

Slagell, Mark. "Ruby User's Guide: Object-Oriented Thinking."
Rubyist, 2008. Retrieved October 30, 2013 (http://
www.rubyist.net/~slagell/ruby/oothinking.html).

Stewart, Bruce. "An Interview with the Creator of Ruby." Linux
DevCenter, November 29, 2001. Retrieved October 27,
2013 (http://www.linuxdevcenter.com/pub/a/linux/
2001/11/29/ruby.html).

St. Laurent, Simon. *Learning Rails 3*. Sebastopol, CA: O'Reilly, 2012.

Techopedia. "IronRuby." 2013. Retrieved October 30,
2013 (http://www.techopedia.com/definition/16397/
ironruby).

Thomas, Dave. *Programming Ruby: The Pragmatic Programmer's Guide*. Raleigh, NC: The Pragmatic Bookshelf, 2005.

Trapani, Gina. "How to Compile Software from Source Code." Lifehacker, July 16, 2008. Retrieved October 30, 2013 (http://lifehacker.com/398611/how-to-compile-software -from-source-code).

Ullman, Larry. *Ruby: Learn Ruby the Quick and Easy Way.* Berkley, CA: Peachpit Press, 2009.

Venners, Bill. "The Philosophy of Ruby: A Conversation with Yukihiro Matsumoto." Artima. Retrieved October 30, 2013 (http://www.artima.com/intv/ruby3.html).

ABOUT THE AUTHOR

Heather Moore Niver is a New York State writer and editor. She has written more than twenty nonfiction books for children, including *Thrill Seekers: Skydivers*, *20 Fun Facts About Stickbugs*, *Tributaries of the Chesapeake*, and *Wild Wheels: Camaros*.

PHOTO CREDITS